REVELATION—
THE LAST BOOK OF THE BIBLE

Edwin A. Schick

REVELATION—

The Last Book of the Bible

FORTRESS PRESS   Philadelphia

Library of Congress Catalog Card Number 76–62602

ISBN 0–8006–1253–1

6189E77   Printed in the United States of America   1–1253

CONTENTS

INTRODUCTION

What in the name of God can we still live by in a shaken and cynical age? What in the name of humanity must we speak out against in the face of rising oppression? Imprisoned on Patmos, John found no way around such questions. He had to meet them head on. In the process he wrote a timely word for the early Christians in Asia Minor. We have this word in the last book of the Bible, the Book of Revelation.

Today's readers respond to John's book in at least three different ways. Some find in it the excitement of incredible prophecies coming true before their very eyes. Through this ancient prophet, they feel, God has provided a blueprint or timetable of world history. As current events fulfill the predictions of long ago we can find out how far we have come on our trip and what distance we have yet to go to reach the end. There is not only excitement but also comfort in knowing this.

Other readers are brought up short by the text of Revelation. The images do not form a coherent picture. The author is felt to be writing on a subject we do not recognize and in a language we do not understand. To make sense of the text seems like an impossible undertaking. We quickly abandon the attempt.

A third group finds John's book less exciting than the first but more comprehensible than the second. To read it, however, is still to experience frustration. A few of its texts speak clearly, while others remain obscure, embedded in the impenetrable sphere of another place and another time.

Some of the excitement of fulfilled prophecy is, I am convinced, a misplaced excitement. Revelation *must* have made sense to its first-century readers. How then can twentieth-century interpreters see in it predictions of contemporary military campaigns in the Mideast or other modern spectaculars such as the explosion of the atomic bomb, or even the organizing of the European Common Market and the World Council of Churches? Such predictions would have been meaningless to the people of the seven churches from Ephesus to Laodicea whom John was addressing.

Furthermore, in my experience the Book of Revelation need not be as difficult or frustrating as some have found it to be. John not only *wanted* to be understood by his first readers; he was in fact understood! He not only *can* be understood today; he *must* be understood! Failure to see with John's eyes results in a reduced vision, the outlook of a world cast adrift and all mixed-up. Such weakened and distorted vision can bring about an equally impoverished life, a life of unreality akin to being afloat on Katherine Ann Porter's *Ship of Fools*.

The chapters of this little book are intended as an aid to understanding the Book of Revelation. I have chosen to follow the "book method" of Bible study. This means four things. First, it means that we go to the New Testament itself and actually read the book.

The Book of Revelation
A Nine-Room Picture Gallery

1. Entrance and Exit, 1:1–8; 22:6–21
2. The Seven Churches and the One Church, 1:9–3:22
3. Thrones and Worship, 4:1–5:14
4. Seven Seals, 6:1–8:1
5. Seven Trumpets, 8:2–11:19
6. Beasts and Church, 12:1–14:20
7. New Exodus, 15:1–16:21
8. The Great City Babylon, 17:1–19:10
9. New Creation, 19:11–22:5

Ours becomes an exploration in Revelation, not a discussion about it. We seriously face the text itself as
we seek to understand what its writer intended to say.
Second, it means that we study the entire text and not
just selected portions of it. We do not have the right to
pick and choose, concentrating only on what we like and
ignoring what may not be so pleasant. Third, it means
that we work with the writing as we have it before us
today. Although the Book of Revelation very likely
went through a long and complicated process years ago
to reach its present form, we will not try to reconstruct
that process. Accordingly, we will not try to rearrange
the verses or passages in the text. Fourth, it means that
we proceed from the general to the specific, from the
book as a whole to any particular segment of it. John's
book is full of pictures, strange but rich images worth
viewing. An overall guide to the gallery as such will
enable us to relate each individual picture to the entire
exhibition. This approach should keep us from getting
lost in the details while also enriching our experience
of the whole—and of the many individual pictures.

John's book can be compared to a building having
nine rooms. We attach no particular significance to the

number nine. This simply appears to be a workable way of dividing up the contents of Revelation. Arrangements geared to the number seven have been tried but are not workable. Early identification of the nine rooms right here at the beginning can help guide us as we move from room to room in the successive chapters that follow.

Before we get into any of the individual rooms, however, we will want to take an overall look at the exposition hall itself. If we can recognize a building from its contours and dimensions, that will enhance our understanding of what goes on inside. It would be a mistake to enter a quiet concert hall expecting to hear a symphony only to discover that we have walked into a noisy gymnasium with a basketball game already in progress. John's building is an apocalypse.

1

APOCALYPSE

Apokalupsis is the very first word of the original Greek text of Revelation. Thus from the very beginning this opening word, "apocalypse," has stood over the last book of the Bible as a kind of book title, the identifying caption of the work. The same word is also used, however, to label a certain *kind* of writing. Here for the first time in the history of literature a book, this last book of the Bible, is called an "apocalypse." In the Latin Bible the same word, translated, reads *revelatio,* "revelation." Today, whether we identify this extraordinary work as the Book of Revelation or as the Apocalypse of John, we mean the same thing. In fact, we mean two things: a specific biblical book *and* a distinctive kind of writing. The Apocalypse is an apocalypse.

John's Greek term has also provided the English-speaking world with another big but useful word. In today's English the word *apocalyptic* carries important meaning and is used with increasing frequency. A quick comparison between our world and John's helps to explain how this came about.

APOCALYPSE AND COVER-UP

The summer of the world exposition in Montreal was also the summer of a tragic riot in Detroit. We remember the glitter of the one and the agony of the other. In his address to the nation after what happened in Detroit—and in other cities across America—President Lyndon Johnson said it as simply and directly as it could be said: "We have endured a week such as no nation should live through, a time of violence and tragedy."[1]   Mayor J. B. Cavanaugh of Detroit said it this way: "But I can't pull the cover over my head and pretend those recent events didn't happen.   That's the way it is with the whole nation.   None of us can pull the cover over our heads any more."[2]

It was the situation which called forth the language, and the language turned out to sound more "apocalyptic" than either speaker may have intended.   When the lid blows off as it did in Detroit that year, or, to use the mayor's metaphor, when the covers are yanked off, we undergo the shock and shame of "revelation."   Our first impulse can only be to "cover up."   Some time after the explosion, however, we begin to wonder what had kept the lid on so long.   There always seems to be resistance to the revealing which cries out to be seen and heard.   The inevitable struggle goes on between apocalypse and cover-up.

In the Hashemite Kingdom of Jordan a few years ago guerrilla forces and King Hussein had come to a bloody showdown.   At the beginning of what was later to be referred to as "black September" the world was introduced to a brand new terror, that of air piracy.   When three hijacked airliners were blown up in the Jordanian desert, and the smoke of the burning wreckage could be seen for twenty-five miles, one reporter covering the event described it as an "apocalyptic scene"[3]—and we knew what he meant.   Once again the lid had blown off, and there was no putting it back on.

Things have changed since the Detroit riot and the Black September hijacking. No one would deny it. But have they really changed? Events that seared into our consciousness the "big lie" and the desperate "cover-up" have their continuing counterparts. War and other horrors seem always as near as the next news telecast. The problems of corruption, enmity, pollution, poverty, hunger, and overpopulation appear staggering—often almost too gruesome to face.

Events and circumstances like these continue to call forth their appropriate terminology. And among the many sounds emerging even in our own language today are continuing echoes from John. An "apocalyptic situation"—that is what one expert has called the situation with respect to world hunger:

> The black horse of famine which rides across the pages of Revelation is not said to be the judgment of God upon the earth. His ravages are the work of man upon himself. Having sown the wind, man reaps the whirlwind. It is one of God's laws, built into the very fabric of creation.[4]

The virtual control of modern industrial technology by large multinational corporations stands, for another writer, as one of the most ominous issues of our time. He too resorts to language from the Book of Revelation when he says that an adequate international reporting and control of these monstrous conglomerates would be "on the order of a millennial vision in today's world."[5]

What was the world situation in which John's millennial vision emerged? What was life like during the thirty years or so which preceded the writing of the biblical Apocalypse?

In the book itself there flash before our eyes pictures of natural disasters such as earthquakes, volcanic eruptions, famines, and epidemics. These function, of course, as symbols for the deeper truths John wants to express, but they fulfill this symbolic function so well precisely because they are also for real. In the year 60–61 a severe earthquake had actually devastated the city of Laodicea, home of one of John's seven churches. In the year 79, after no less than sixteen years of threats and rumbling, Mount Vesuvius had finally exploded in the most dramatic volcanic eruption of all time. Three cities ringing the Bay of Naples, including the famous Pompeii, were buried by its molten lava. So awesome was the catastrophe that one of the Latin poets, Martial, pictured the gods themselves wishing they had not been allowed to go this far! In the year 92 a grain famine proved severe enough to force the Roman Emperor Domitian to decree a reduction of acreage for vineyards in order to allow for a possible increase in the yields of grain. It was very likely during the administration of this same Domitian that the seer of Revelation wrote his book. So it is not surprising that natural disasters of epic proportion find their way into his imagery.

In the text of Revelation there flash before our eyes, however, other pictures as well, pictures from the world of politics and the military. Again, they function effectively as symbols of profounder realities precisely because they originate in actual experience. In the year 62 the invincible Roman army on the eastern frontier had suffered a humiliating defeat at the hands of the Parthians, and no matter how bad the Romans from the west may have appeared to the early Christian believers, who could have been at ease with a Parthian threat from the east? In July of 64 uncontrolled fires raged for days in Rome and left most of the city in ashes; the emperor Nero responded with devilish ordeals for the Christians. In 66 another hell broke loose with the Jewish revolt against the Romans; it ended four years later with a Roman victory and the capture and destruction of Jerusalem. In 68 Nero committed suicide; near political chaos resulted, with no less than four emperors succeeding to the throne during the course of a single year.

"Apocalypse" may still look and sound like an odd word. Revelation may yet turn out to be a strange book. However, that which we have in common with the world of John and the churches in Asia Minor surely gives us a place to start. When we open the Book of Revelation we hear immediately at least an echo of the familiar. One of the best English commentators on the Book of Revelation begins his great commentary with these words: "If we make adequate allowance for vast technological change, the times John lived in were astonishingly like our own, perhaps more so than any of the intervening centuries."[6] Our brief glance at the two histories almost twenty centuries apart has served to verify this conclusion. A reporter can describe the modern scene as "apocalyptic." An authority on hunger can refer to the world food situation today as "apocalyptic." Their term is deliberately chosen: it comes from the last book of the Bible, which begins with the word *apocalypse*.

While we have found some important familiar ground between John's time and our own, however, this does not prove that the language we share with him necessarily means the same thing in both worlds. It could mean no more than that our modern usage has an ancient ancestry. Can we pin down the word *apocalypse* with greater precision?

"Apocalypse" (at least as it applies to the Book of

Daniel in the Old Testament and the Book of Revelation in the New Testament) has reference to both content and form: the special kind of explosive content which speaks to a critical situation, and the particular form of symbolism or picture language in which this content is expressed. To put it in the terms of the scholars, apocalypse functions both as a category of doctrine and as a category of literature. More simply put, the term refers to both message and method, both *what* we say and *how* we say it. We turn first to the content and then to the form.

APOCALYPSE AND POLITICS

In as direct a way as can be found anywhere apocalypse raises the political question, Who is Lord? And not only who *is,* but who *will be* Lord, and *when*? An intense interest in the future accompanies the political issue. God rules. His kingdom has come. But so long as the earthly tyrant has his say there remains a crucially urgent question; timing is critical. When is the kingdom of God really coming?

When the earthly trinity of political, military, and economic-industrial power becomes a unity with its own subservient priesthood, what kind of monstrous tyranny can this represent? The dragon and the two beasts of Revelation 12 and 13 provide an answer. When this power puts itself on a collision course with the sovereignty of God, what happens then? The fall of Babylon in Revelation 18 speaks to that. Who is Lord? Is it Antiochus Epiphanes and the Syrian state at the time of the Maccabees in the second century B.C., or is it the Ancient of Days with his saints of the Most High? Daniel 7 responds with a clear voice. Who is Lord of lords and King of kings in John's day, the emperor Domitian and the Roman state or God and his Christ? The blast of the seventh trumpet in Revelation 11 leaves the answer in no doubt.

Political roll call for the people of the Bible starts as far back as the Assyrian conquest in the ninth century B.C. and continues through the Roman rule of the first century A.D. For the earlier prophetic voices of Amos, Hosea, Micah, and the early Isaiah it was the Assyrians who posed a threat to the Lord's sovereignty; for Jeremiah and Ezekiel it was the Babylonians; for the prophet of the Exile it was the Persians (though in a more positive way). For the more distinctly apocalyptic voice of Zechariah it was the Greeks, and for Daniel it was the Syrians. For the people of Qumran by the Dead Sea, for John and the seven churches of Asia Minor addressed in the Book of Revelation, and for the writers of the ancient nonbiblical apocalypses of 2 Esdras and 2 Baruch it was the Romans. In every age God's people have had to confront and come to terms with political power.

Evil provides a corollary to the political question. For the apocalyptic mind, when powerful people are also wicked evil breaks out in ways far worse than we could ever expect. We had no idea it could be this bad! In this respect apocalypse stands for the shock of recognition. On the other hand, when evil has done its worst, or even while it is still doing it, the apocalyptic vision sees God asserting his sovereignty. He remains more powerful, more in control than we could possibly fathom. The mightier the assault of wickedness, the greater the revealing of God as having the last word. The more overwhelming the feeling of human helplessness and hopelessness, the greater the assurance of God's active role and final say. In this respect apocalypse stands for faith becoming certain not because of the presence of evidence but in spite of its absence.

So long as God occupies the throne as the Ancient of Days it cannot be the Syrian state of Antiochus Epiphanes but the saints of the Most High who receive the kingdom (Daniel 7). This message is what made Daniel an apocalyptic book in the political crisis of the second century B.C., when loyal Jews were given the choice of denying their faith or having their throats cut. When the seventh trumpet blows, the pastor on Patmos hears the kingdom of the world becoming the kingdom of the Lord and of his Christ (Revelation 11:15). The preaching of this truth makes the Book of Revelation an apocalyptic book toward the close of the first century A.D., when Christians face beheading unless they confess Caesar as Lord. The two keys are essentially the same. They unlock the entrance to that basic content of apocalyptic which makes it so distinctive: in face of the appalling disclosure of massive, haughty, and unchecked evil God is *and remains* sovereign!

REVELATION THROUGH PICTURES

Apocalyptic, as we have said, is not only a matter of content. It is distinctive also in form. Apocalyptic form means no more and no less than that symbolism has been chosen as the most appropriate language. This may take some getting used to on our part, though a generation attuned to the vibrancy of today's multimedia communication should experience no great difficulty. In Revelation we encounter a variety of visions and colorful symbols. We meet numbers and animals and angels. We see lightning and hear thunder. There are earthquakes and battles and the hallelujah chorus. We see the sparkle of jewels and a woman clothed with the sun facing a terrifying dragon. We hear the music of harps, and smell the smell of sulfur.

John's pictures are intended to evoke an emotional response in depth. We get into trouble when we try to reconstruct them rationally in literal detail, when we let the medium obscure the message. He places the symbol before us and invites us not only to look at it but also to look *through* it, to see the reality it discloses. To see what the symbol stands for is to experience the light, sometimes also the shock, of recognition. When the point of the symbol comes through we can be stirred to the depth of our being. Rather he invites us to enter into the miracle of atonement and forgiveness, and this in a setting of martyrdom.

Picture language need not be all that difficult. When John pictures the robes washed white in the blood of the lamb (7:14) he does not require us to concoct a fantastic kind of chemistry by which garments soaked in blood come out white.

To question how the human figure who is more than a human (1:12–20) can speak at all while he has a sword coming out of his mouth is simply to miss the point. It would be equally obtuse to ask how his right hand can be laid on John even while it holds in its grasp the seven stars. An approach like this would be about as unresponsive to reality as the person (described by Martin Luther) who reacts to the wonders of nature with all the dullness of "a cow staring at a new gate." Something more imaginative will be asked of us on our study tour of Revelation.

2

ENTRANCE AND EXIT

As we pause at the entry way we note that we stand also at the exit. Our way in will be our way out. A number of features common to the introduction to the book (1:1–8) and to its conclusion (22:6–21) make this a double doorway.

ALPHA AND OMEGA

Alpha and Omega belong to the first things we see as we enter (1:8) and to the last as we leave (22:13). We see the words once more in between (21:6). Here John has done something no other writer in the Bible did. He joined the first and last letters of the Greek alphabet into a symbolic expression. It sounds more elegant in Greek, but in plain English it means "from A to Z." None other than the Lord God Almighty reveals himself at the beginning as "the Alpha and the Omega," the one "who is and who was and who is to come" (1:8). At the end, the coming Lord refers to himself as "the Alpha and the Omega, the first and the last, the beginning and the end" (22:13). People attentive to John cannot doubt in whose presence they stand. The book comes from John, but the revelation comes from God who is there from A to Z and at all points between.

"I JOHN"

As with Alpha and Omega, John introduces himself by name as we enter (1:1, 4) and as we leave (22:8), and a third time within (1:9). John who? We have no way of giving a sure answer. A leading candidate would be John the disciple, one of the twelve. However, if he is the author of Revelation then the traditional author of the Gospel and of the Epistles of John must be someone else. The recent proposal that the "I John" of the Book of Revelation is John the Baptist remains just that, a proposal.

His name was John. The churches in Asia Minor recognized him. Beyond this we can say little about his precise identity. Considerably more can be said about him as a person. On the basis of his opening word we have already met John as the author of an apocalypse. Standing in the doorway we now meet him in his additional roles of letter writer, prophet, and pastor.

John addresses the seven churches. As expected of a letter writer he follows the opening identification of himself and of those addressed with the familiar "Grace to you and peace" (1:4). At the close "I Jesus" puts himself behind what "I John" has said (22:8,16). The final sentence of the book becomes the closing formula of a letter: "The grace of the Lord Jesus be with all the saints" (22:21). What John writes he sends in its entirety to the seven congregations from Ephesus to Laodicea (1:11). In addition each of the seven receives its own letter (chapters 2 and 3). John composes an apocalypse but he adopts the letter form to do it. The seven letters to the seven churches alone would make him one of the most famous letter writers in all of literature.

In addition John qualifies as a prophet. Like a prophet he gets right to the point: "Blest is the reader of these words of prophecy, and blest are those who hear and heed them" (1:3). He reaffirms the blessing at the end in almost identical terms (22:7). Here, however, a curse accompanies it: "Curst will be anyone who tampers with the book either by way of adding to or subtracting from its words of prophecy" (22:18,19). In addition, the nearness of the time means that the words of the prophecy of John's book are not to be sealed up (22:10). Twice more in the conclusion John sounds the prophetic note. His Lord is "the God of the spirits of the prophets" (22:6), and the revealing angel puts him into the fellowship of servants and prophets (22:9). In this surpassing fashion at the beginning and the end (and there are several more references to prophets within) John shows his great respect for the order of prophets and numbers himself among them. His scroll turns out to be the preeminent prophetic book of the New Testament.

To be an apocalyptist, a letter writer, and a prophet all rolled into one would seem to be enough for any one person. For John, however, one more thing needs to be said. If John were asked, he would probably say, "Yes, I am all that. I am an apocalyptist, a letter writer, and a prophet. Yet I am none of these. What I really am is a pastor, a shepherd to some of the great flock of God." Admittedly the late Middle English word "pastor" would not be in John's vocabulary. Nevertheless the pastor's robe fits him well. "John to the seven churches" at the beginning (1:4) and "I John" at the end (22:8)—

this is all the introduction he needs. In 1:9 he adds "I John, your brother." He claims the right to be heard but does not bestow upon himself any title of "apostle" or "elder" or "bishop" to shore up his position. "On the Lord's day" (understood as Sunday) the pastor on Patmos feels his lonely exile particularly keenly. "In the Spirit" (1:10) he is given to see what others cannot see. What he sees and hears become his privilege and his burden, and above all his pastoral calling.

URGENCY

As we continue looking around in the doorway, John presses upon us his feeling of urgency. Something is about to happen. Revelation is given to Jesus Christ so that he can in turn (through his angel and John) show to his people "what must soon take place" (1:1), and these identical words suggestive of imminent occurrence appear again at the end (22:6). At the beginning we hear the blessing spoken to both the reader of the text and the hearers of it who choose also to heed because "the time is near" (1:3), and at the end we find John under orders not to seal up his writing (as in a time capsule for future discovery) because "the time is near" (22:10). In both instances *The New English Bible* translates the word for time as "the hour of fulfilment." By inscribing these two pairs of identical phrases in his double doorway John has made his point inescapably sharp: things are about to happen!

To consider the exit once more, we hear three identical promises by the Lord to come soon. First, "And behold I am coming soon" (22:7). Then again, "Behold, I am coming soon" (22:12), this time with the additional promise (or is it a threat?) to repay them all according to their due. Finally, in what is almost its parting word the book quotes: "Surely I am coming soon" (22:20); only the yearning response, "Amen. Come Lord Jesus!" and the benediction follow (22:21).

Urgency and not complacency, nearness and not distance—these are the sentinels posted by John at the boundaries of his work. What kind of nearness do they represent? What is there to be urgent about? A number of answers have been given, each laying claim to being the correct one.

One answer turns to the past, that is, our past but John's present. A church under pressure from a hostile power provides the writer of Revelation with his feeling of urgency. The hour of persecution is at hand. The political question which we will later hear raised to a high note we hear raised in a low key in both the introduction and the conclusion. Jesus Christ is said at the outset to be "the ruler of kings on earth" (1:5); he has "made us a kingdom" (1:6). The last of the seven blessings in the book reads, "Blessed are those who wash their robes" (22:14). Washing robes refers to martyrdom. While history cannot repeat itself exactly, it does repeat. Later readers in circumstances similar to those of John's day find his message equally urgent.

Another answer concentrates on the present, that is, our present but John's future. This interpretation (as we saw earlier) finds in Revelation the story of world history. The story becomes alive when people see the predictions of Revelation come true in their own time. The higher the correlation between prophecy and fulfilment the greater the miracle of inspiration and the more urgent the message. The number 666 in Revelation 13:18 has always had its peculiar fascination. Examples galore, funny if they were not also pathetic, could be given of the number's present fulfilment in whatever terms the interpreter finds congenial. In Reformation polemics the number stood for either the Reformers or the Papacy, depending upon which side you were on. In a national election the number could stand for either Franklin D. Roosevelt or Herbert Hoover, again depending upon which party you belonged to.

A third answer looks to the future, not only John's future but our future and the future of all who live before the close of history. Urgency becomes synonymous with imminence. The hour is at hand, not of a critical historical happening but of the supreme event at the end itself when the Lord returns to dissolve the first heaven and earth for the new. On "the Lord's day" (understood not as Sunday but as the future "Day of the Lord" of the prophets) John is transported to the time of the end (1:10). There he sees not only what the end will be like but possibly also when it will take place. This is now what the Book of Revelation is all about according to the futurists. The symbols become pictures of the end.

Where the first three interpretations have linked themselves to particular points on the time line, a fourth position rests on an essential timelessness in John's symbolism. It holds that symbols tied too closely to calendar dates become the servants and not the masters of time and thus cease being symbols. This fourth answer finds predictions of the end not only fruitless but boring. It finds in Revelation a different kind of urgency altogether. Imminence means not that the *end* is here but that the *Lord* comes near, now and always.

In the midst of variables such as these, two constants remain: First, if John or the early church or both understood "the time is near" or "I am coming soon" to mean the imminence of the end, then obviously they were in error; that end has not come in 2000 years and for all we know may not come in the next 2000. Nevertheless, the church has prayed "Amen. Come, Lord Jesus!" (22:20) not for a few early years or decades but for twenty centuries; it has never quit praying this prayer of the end and is not about to quit now. This is the second constant. Together they mean that while John was wrong or was misunderstood on some things, he was also ultimately and profoundly correct. For the church not to see what John saw could spell disaster.

Thus far we have remained standing in a double doorway. With our jumping back and forth between introduction and conclusion it may have seemed more like a revolving door. Whatever the case, we are now ready to move on. As we do so we are tempted to ask the real John to stand up. Is he interpretation number one or two or three or four? Or all of them? Or none of them? A great revealing awaits us in the gallery itself.

3

THE SEVEN CHURCHES AND
THE ONE CHURCH

Seeing and hearing figure prominently in Revelation, and must also in our dealing with it. John says "I saw" forty-five times in the book and "I heard" twenty-seven times. To follow John therefore means to move through his picture gallery seeing and hearing. In the room we now enter we participate in the birth of a prophet as John sees and hears the Lord (1:9–20), and in the private yet public life of seven congregations in Asia Minor (chapters 2 and 3). These two pictures fuse in a way to become the symbol of the seven churches and the one church.

BIRTH OF A PROPHET

"In the spirit on the Lord's day" John hears behind him a voice like a trumpet blast. Turning around he sees seven lamps of gold (the seven churches) and in their midst "one like a son of man" (the Lord himself). In priestly attire the Lord radiates a splendor which knocks John to the ground. The words "Fear not" restore him, and he follows the directive to write to each of these seven congregations (1:9–20).

Almost too quickly for us to grasp, an inaugural vision has turned into the commissioning of a prophet in the honored tradition of Old Testament prophets, especially the prophet Ezekiel. By the river Chebar, Ezekiel received his vision of the throne-chariot, the famous "wheel within a wheel." Overcome by this "appearance of the likeness of the glory of the Lord" Ezekiel fell upon his face only to be spoken to as "son of man" and ordered to get back on his feet. The Spirit entered into him, set him on his feet, and thus a prophetic career was born (Ezek. 1:1–2:7).

Now on Patmos (Rev. 1:12–20) John is overwhelmed by the appearance of "one like a son of man" and falls before him in a dead faint. With the laying on of the majestic figure's right hand John hears the command, "Now write what you see, what is and what is to take place hereafter." Thus is born the career of a New Testament prophet. Later on in the book—though not necessarily "later" in John's life—and again in the manner of Ezekiel, John receives a scroll to eat, sweet to taste but bitter to digest, with another commission to "prophesy about many peoples and nations and tongues and kings" (10:11).

In the entry way we met John as a prophet. In this room we see the birthing experience which made him that.

SEVEN LETTERS

John hears an order to keep a record of what he sees and to send it to the seven congregations which are specifically named. All seven are to get the entire scroll (1:11). As part of the scroll John writes an individual letter to each of the seven (chapters 2 and 3). The result is seven private letters which cease being private when seen by the other six.

These famous letters to the seven churches have a common structure: (1) an address to the angel of the congregation named, (2) a detail from the preceding picture of the "one like a son of man" which serves to identify the one addressing the congregation as the Lord himself, (3) the comforting or threatening claim that the Lord knows exactly what is going on in the life of the congregation, (4) an evaluation of that life of the congregation, (5) an exhortation to the congregation growing out of the evaluation, (6) an admonition to hear what the Spirit says to the churches, and (7) a promise held out to the one who gains the victory. This is the order in the first three letters; in the next four, items 5 and 6 are reversed as a subtle hint that for John the number 7 is not a static one. There are seven letters but they come in two groups of three and four.

Several of the common features of these letters warrant a closer look. Item 1 designates the letter as written to the church (singular) in a particular city; item 6 calls upon the individual congregation to pay attention to what the Spirit says to the churches (plural). In the introductory picture we saw the Lord "in the midst of" or "among" the seven lamps (1:13). In the first letter, the one to Ephesus, we see him "walking among" the lamps (2:1). Already the intimacy of the Lord's relation to the churches has been established. In addition, item 2 by repeating a different detail of this earlier picture for each of the seven congregations continues this motif of intimacy. Finally, item 3 quotes the Lord as saying "I know," not "we know" or "they know," but "I know." There are not many lords but one Lord. From all this we can come to at least one firm conclusion: Any one letter or all seven together ought never be

read in isolation from the preceding picture of the
Lord (1:12–20). The picture of the Lord of the church
and the individual pictures of the seven congregations
have merged to form one symbol. The seven churches
are the one church.

ONE CHURCH

John pulls the covers off the private lives of seven
different congregations in first-century Asia Minor.
These churches are real, not imaginary. They are real
enough to have their sites become the objects of archaeo-
logical investigation. Ephesus, Pergamum, and Sardis
have been studied with some thoroughness. At least
five of the seven congregations (probably not Thyatira
and Laodicea) had to live out their Christian life in
centers where the pressures of emperor worship were
intense. The political question for them was not theo-
retical but actual.

These real churches, however, are also symbolic.
John addresses seven of them, no more and no less, and
we experience no difficulty with the number seven as a
symbol of the oneness and completeness of the church.
Why just these seven when other congregations were
doubtless also available? We can only conjecture. Perhaps these seven most adequately portrayed the total
church. The whole church embraces the strengths of
Philadelphia and Smyrna as well as the weaknesses of
Sardis and Laodicea. However Ephesus, Pergamum,
and Thyatira also belong, being neither as strong as the
former nor as weak as the latter.

The letter form of John's apocalypse has made its
point. Not only Thyatira but "all the churches" shall
know that it is the Son of God who with his flaming

eyes "searches mind and heart" and reacts accordingly (2:23). The church cannot be solely the one or the other but must be all seven put together. The one cannot disown the others and the others cannot disown the one as together they stand under the scrutiny of the Lord and of each other. Under the Lord and in their full disclosure to each other the seven churches become the one church.

WHAT THE SEVEN LETTERS ARE NOT

However, a quite different truth has also been seen in the symbol of the seven letters, namely a prediction of the seven periods of church history. A renowned student of the Book of Revelation concluded, "Only the most perverse ingenuity can treat the messages to the seven churches as directly prophetical."[7] Nevertheless this kind of ingenuity has not been as rare as one might think. One scheme of the prophetic timetable goes like this: Ephesus is a picture of the first-century apostolic church; Smyrna stands for the persecuted church of the first three centuries; Pergamum is the church from 323 to 800 (from Constantine to Charlemagne); Thyatira stands for the church from 800 to 1294 (the year Boniface VIII became Pope); Sardis becomes the church from 1294 to the beginning of the Reformation in 1517; Philadelphia then stands for the church of the Reformation to the end of the seventeenth century; Laodicea portrays the church of the last time up to the end.[8]

The interpreter of course has given himself away. He has to stand in the Reformation tradition, or how else could he have come to the conclusion that the highly complimented congregation in Philadelphia portrays the "blessed" Reformation, as he calls it? It is the besetting shortcoming of the "fulfilled prophecy" kind of interpretation to end up in this bind. Invariably the good predictions apply to oneself, the bad ones to others. The symbol serves to reflect little more than the "what-a-good-boy-am-I" face of the beholder.

4

THRONES AND WORSHIP

The last of the seven letters has been read. Laodicea has heard the victory-promise of a share in the throne of the Lord just as the Lord shares in the Father's throne (3:21). This throne room of God becomes the setting for room number three in John's gallery. In the intimacy of holiness the earthly and the heavenly find their togetherness, and the pastoral heart of John shows itself as a liturgical heart.

The picture soars in worship. We have entered the great throne room and see God himself on the throne. The flashing of colorful jewelry best portrays his majesty (4:1–6a). A Lamb enters the scene, powerful (the seven horns) and taking it all in (the seven eyes). There he stands as though slain. Though unmistakably alive again, he still shows the marks of having been killed in sacrifice (5:6).

THE CONGREGATION

A large and diverse congregation gathers for worship. Twenty-four elders come first. Dignified with age, robed in white, and crowned with gold they sit on their own thrones (4:4). For their identification we need to pick up a clue which comes later. In the wall of the holy city Jerusalem there are twelve gates, and on the gates are the names of the twelve tribes of the sons of Israel (21:12). The wall of the city has twelve foundations, and on the foundations are the names of the twelve apostles of the Lamb (21:14). If the twenty-four elders do not represent these twelve tribes and twelve apostles then we are at a bit of a loss as to how to account for them. The former Israel and the later Israel, God's people in their entirety, become in the persons of the twenty-four elders the first important part of the congregation.

Four living creatures come next, animal figures described in turn as resembling a lion, an ox, a human being, and a flying eagle (4:6–8). They represent all of living creation, not only people but three other kinds of creatures too: wild animals, tame animals, and birds. While we may hesitate to ascribe to them any act of devotion to their creator, John has no such hesitation.

Finally there come the angelic hosts without number, "myriads of myriads and thousands of thousands" (5:11). These three groups make up the congregation: elders, living creatures, and angelic hosts. Their liturgy moves in an orderly progression of five hymns.

THE HYMNS

The worship begins as we hear the four representatives of creation singing the first hymn of tribute to the holiness of God (4:8). To say that this "begins" the liturgy is of course awkward. Where does it begin when the creatures offer their worship constantly day and night?

Nevertheless, as the creatures sing, the twenty-four elders fall before the throne, remove their crowns, and in their own second hymn proclaim the worthiness and glory of God because he created all things (4:10,11). Twice in one breath John describes this creator God as the one "who lives for ever and ever" (4:9,10). How does one express the eternal? The Greeks do it by saying "into the ages of the ages." Encountered already in 1:6 and 1:18, the expression will be repeated many more times.

The worship moves to its third stage. God has in his right hand a scroll with seven seals. No one except the Lamb has the qualifications to unseal the scroll, and he takes it from the hand of God. The four creatures and the twenty-four elders together (not separately as before) now worship the Lamb who by his blood has ransomed people for God and has turned them into a priestly kingdom (5:9,10). This combined choir sings "a new song"—new because it was not possible before but is possible now in the new time of the Lamb and his sacrifice. This makes it for John a Christian celebration.

We look some more and hear the voice of unnumbered angels in a fourth song (5:11,12). Theirs becomes a loud voice in praise of the worthiness of the slain Lamb. Words pile up; they can hardly come fast enough. Power, wealth, wisdom, might, honor, glory, and blessing—the Lamb deserves all seven!

The fifth hymn becomes the climax. All creatures in heaven and earth and under the earth and in the sea and everything in them join in singing their special hymn (5:13,14). All of these (and it would be hard to be more inclusive) bring the heavenly liturgy to its highest point by directing their worship to both God and the Lamb. Everlastingly, blessing and honor and glory and might belong to both. The creatures say "Amen," and the elders fall down and worship (5:14). "Amen" and "worship," these are the closing words. What else can one say? At least for the pastor on Patmos the mystery of God and his ways is such that worship alone can afford access to it.

WORSHIP AND POLITICAL POWER

The pressure of the holy has for John become irresistible. Of course he has not forgotten, and will not permit us to forget, that much of the world is not only not interested in this worship business but stands in fierce opposition to it. He can, however, hardly be blamed for his ideal picture of full response to an all-encompassing holiness.

Keep politics out of worship? John would not have understood the question. The political overtones of his picture are unmistakable. Whom do we worship, God or Caesar; the conquering Lion of the tribe of Judah (5:5) who promptly turns into a Lamb (5:6), or a quite different kind of power?

Two words deserve our attention before we move on. "Throne" dominates the scene, occurring no less than nineteen times in chapters 4 and 5, twice in the plural as the thrones of the elders but seventeen times in the singular as the throne of God. This throne of God stands in direct contrast to the throne of Satan (2:13)—a reference to emperor worship—the throne of the beast (13:2), and the throne of the dragon (16:10). Altogether John mentions a throne forty-six times in his book.

As we have already seen, "worship" concludes the scene (5:14). John uses the verb *worship* twenty-four times in Revelation. The worship of God and the Lamb has its opposite in another kind of devotion, especially in the politically explosive chapter 13. There the worship of the dragon (13:4), of the beast (13:4,8, 12), and of the image of the beast (13:15) receive full attention. Five more times we are told about the worship of the beast and his image (14:9,11; 16:2; 19:20; 20:4).

Throne and worship dominate the picture. John has made his point.

5

SEVEN SEALS

The scroll with its seven seals and the Lamb who alone has the right to unseal it leave an unforgettable impression. Entering the next room we see the Lamb moving into action. He takes off the seals one by one. The action, however, is not a mechanical movement from one to seven. The first four pictures form the unit of "the four horsemen of the apocalypse," one of the best known of all of John's symbols. Numbers five and six follow directly, but number seven has to wait for the portrayal of the sealed multitude in their heavenly perfection. Again John's seven is not a static one. Where in reference to the seven churches it was three and four, here it is four, two, and one.

FOUR HORSEMEN

Who are the four galloping horses with their riders (6:1–8)? In popular usage they have come to stand for just about anything, ranging from a famous backfield in football to the ordinary woes which daily beset us. In a cartoon of "The Better Half" series the husband, clad in pajamas and half asleep at the breakfast table, moans, "I wonder if the Four Horsemen of the Apocalypse don't ever get bored playing with me."[9] Another cartoon has considerably more substance. Four black-robed skeletons come galloping down the street on their four black horses. One of them carries a scythe. As they bear down on us, a man in a business suit turns to a uniformed doorman and says, "Let's hope they're on their way to a masquerade party."[10]

The first of John's four riders sits on a white horse, holds a bow, receives a crown, and moves from conquest to conquest. The title of the picture therefore is *conquest,* representing most immediately for the Asian Christians the threat of the Parthian invader from the east. The bow provides the basis for this interpretation. So characteristic of the Parthian forces was the bow, and so expert did they become in fighting on horseback with the bow as their only weapon, that "Parthian shot" has become part of the English language. The expression comes from the skill of the Parthians to use their bows and arrows even in retreat.

John's second rider, mounted on a red horse, takes peace from the earth and wields a big sword. The name in this instance is *war.* Where the white horse gallops to conquest from without, the red one gallops to civil war within. This appears to be the meaning of killing "one another."

The rider of the third horse, a black one, carries a pair of scales. Here the name is a double one, *famine* and *poverty,* with grain priced high and in short supply for the have-nots and the luxury of oil and wine for those who have. A more incisive reference to the rich becoming richer and the poor becoming poorer would be hard to find.

Appropriately, the last of the four riders sits on a pale horse. Pale stands for a yellowish green, or whatever color can best suggest death. The name is clearly *death,* with the *grave* (or Hades) tagging along behind.

As we look at these four horsemen what do we see? For one thing, we see a description. The symbol portrays things as they are. Statistics on war, famine, and disease can be shrugged off. So John gives us the shock treatment of a symbol. The way we react emotionally to the symbol becomes the way we are to react to what is symbolized. The horsemen seem not so much to be galloping off as to be bearing down on us. They overpower us with the facts of invasion, civil strife, famine, poverty, disease, and death. Thus the symbol forces a recognition of what has been there all the time. Now we see what before we had conveniently covered up.

However, we see more than simply an effective description of what we should be quite capable of seeing by ourselves. We see also revelation of truth about God beyond our ordinary seeing. The symbol participates in the reality it expresses by pointing beyond itself. We look no longer *at* the symbol but *through* it to the truth behind and beyond it. Through these riders we see two realities uncovered.

First, you cannot beat the system. People have to pay the price of wrong choices, whether their own or somebody else's. Satan is not absent in the Book of Revelation, but these four riders are neither the devil nor his evil angels. They ride as human beings representing our own misdeeds. The horsemen do their work as the inevitable consequences of wrong decisions made earlier. People are in charge, but not absolutely. It is God's scroll which the Lamb unseals. Evil deeds have evil consequences. That is the system, and because God is God we cannot beat it.

Through the symbol of the horsemen we come to see a second truth. God is absolutely in charge, but not yet. God and his Christ have the final say. The Book of Revelation is clear on that. But between now and that final word there can be much freedom for evil and much arbitrariness. Evil deeds and evil consequences do not proceed in a one-to-one correspondence. The innocent suffer and are destroyed; the guilty escape and prosper. John may even have in mind that specific war, poverty, and death which is inflicted upon the followers of the Lamb by virtue of the fact that they dare to follow him. By removing the seals the Lamb releases these afflictions as the price to be paid by those who dare to take up their cross and follow their Messiah.[11]

The four horsemen are not on the way to a masquerade party. They are for real; let's face it.

FROM DESPAIR TO HOPE

As the fourth rider leaves the scene, the Lamb takes off the fifth seal. The martyrs now have their chance to express their impatience in waiting for God's verdict to be given (6:9–11). They are told to rest a bit longer, the great day of wrath comes quickly enough. With the sixth seal removed, disasters come pouring forth in awesome profusion—violent earthquake, blackened sun, bloodied moon, fallen stars and rolled-up sky, mountains and islands moved away (6:12–17). In this great day of the wrath of God and of the Lamb all people, from kings to slaves, rush to hide in caves and among the rocks. They cry out in despair: "Who can stand?" (6:17).

The question of despair receives its answer of hope

in the interlude between the sixth and seventh seals (called "interlude" by us and not by John). There are those who can stand, not only the 144,000 sealed with the seal of God, but the vast throng, much too large to be numbered, who are dressed in robes made white in the blood of the Lamb and who serve God in his temple day and night (chapter 7).

The breaking of the seventh seal brings an unexpected and unusual silence, unexpected after the ongoing fullness we have become accustomed to and unusual in that this becomes the silence of both sound and sight. We hear nothing and see nothing for approximately half an hour (8:1). For us to intrude upon this silence in a chattering attempt to explain it would be inexcusable. Let us simply accept it for what it is—silence.

6

SEVEN TRUMPETS

The half hour of silence has lasted about as long as one can stand total silence. A double reference at the entrance (8:2,6) not only announces what there is to see and hear in the next room, but also frames the picture of answered prayer (8:3–5) as an introduction to the seven angels and their seven trumpets (8:7–11:19).

An angel has taken his place at the altar with a gold incense pot. He receives a liberal supply of incense to add to the prayers of God's people, and both the smoke of the incense and the prayers ascend together. The angel then fills his censer with fire from the altar and throws it on the earth where the effects are startling—thunder and noises and lightning and an earthquake (8:3–5). There is nothing mysterious about this. It is a symbolic way of saying that God answers prayer. Instead of writing an essay on the subject John paints a picture. When the saints pray, God hears—and things happen.

ONE-THIRD

After this energetic preparation the six angels blow their trumpets one by one. As they do so the number one-third enters to play its important role. All of the sixteen occurrences of this fraction in the New Testament are found in the Book of Revelation, and fifteen of them are in the scene before us. The sounding of the first four trumpets bring calamities in turn upon one-third of the earth, sea, fresh water, and sky—a clear reminder of the plagues in Egypt at the time of Moses and the Exodus.

What does John mean by the one-third? The number is sizable enough to become a great threat to the security of the remaining two-thirds. As the sixth trumpet sounds, one-third of mankind is killed but the other two-thirds fail to repent of their idolatry and cruelty (9:18–21). "The calamities destroy the security of human existence, but they do not make up the whole of God's judgment; they serve as a warning, inviting men to repentance."[12] As in Egypt so in Rome the warning goes unheeded.

Trumpets five and six are separated from the first four by the announcement in 8:13 of the three "woes" yet to come, and are removed from trumpet number seven by the interlude in chapters 10 and 11 and the special announcement of the passing of the second woe in 11:14.

The fifth angel now blows his trumpet. From the mouth of the abyss smoke comes pouring out, enough to darken the sun, and from the smoke locusts come over the earth with the sting of scorpions. The locusts have power, but God has very definitely limited that power. Their area of jurisdiction does not include the grass or any green growth or tree; it covers only those among mankind who have not been sealed as God's own people, and over these the locusts have only the power to cause pain but not to kill. The time limit of their authority is five months (9:1–6). The army of locusts becomes an army of horses commanded by the angel of the abyss, in Hebrew Abaddon, in Greek Apollyon, in English "the Destroyer." These horses too can sting like scorpions, and again the time for them to hurt people is limited to five months (9:7–11). What in the first instance amounts to the life-span of a locust (more or less five months) becomes a symbol affirming the power of God and no one else to set the limits.

This sole authority of God to set the limits is also an integral part of the picture of the sixth trumpet (9:13–21). Four angels had been bound at the river Euphrates, held in reserve for this very hour and day and month and year (9:15). Now they are released for the killing of one-third of mankind. With this act there becomes explicit what may already have been implicit in the preceding picture of locusts and cavalry. We are on the eastern frontier of the Roman empire facing the threat of an invasion by the Parthians from across the Euphrates. Suddenly the cavalry becomes impossibly huge, twice 10,000 times 10,000. But exaggeration and symbolic enumeration is the apocalyptic way. For us to approach it in prosaic literalness would be to limp when we ought to soar.

THREE YEARS AND A HALF

The interlude between trumpets six and seven (10:1–11:13) becomes an important second part of the present vision. The early part of this interlude (chapter 10) we have noted before: the mighty angel with the little scroll for John to eat, announcing the imminent coming of the big event of the seventh trumpet. It is particularly the reference to three and one-half years in the portrayal of the two witnesses in 11:1–13 which now demands our careful attention. It demands attention because it functions as an important test case for the historical versus the prophetic interpretation of the Book of Revelation. We will consider the historical interpretation first and return to the prophetic later.

John receives an unexpected order to measure the temple and its altar and those worshipping there but to exclude from his measurements the court outside. This court belongs to the Gentiles and they will stomp on the Holy City for forty-two months (11:1,2). At the same time God empowers his two witnesses to prophesy for 1260 days (11:3). The period of the Gentiles and of the witnesses is therefore the same, three and one-half years, a year reckoned as twelve months of thirty days each. The two witnesses have the power to shut the sky, so that no rain can fall during this time of prophesying, and the power to turn water into blood and to produce plagues (11:6). Consequently there can be little doubt about their identity being broad enough to include the figures of Elijah and Moses. At the end of their testimony, that is, at the end of three and one-half years, the beast from the abyss murders the two witnesses and their corpses lie unburied in the street of the city (Sodom and Egypt and Jerusalem all rolled in one). For three and one-half days the good riddance of the obnoxious witnesses is celebrated only to have the corpses come to life after three and one-half days and ascend to heaven in full view of their foes.

The number three and one-half stands out as an important designation. It is used specifically for the three and one-half days, which designation however does not occur again. But the time of three and one-half years

(forty-two months, 1260 days) is m
chapter 13, where two beasts do th
ceives power from the dragon to
thority for forty-two months, nam
to wage a winning war against u..
over all whose names are not recorded in
book of life (13:1-10). In chapter 12, where the u.
gon is foiled in his attempt to devour the child born of
the woman clothed with the sun, the child is caught up
to the throne of God and the woman escapes into the
wilderness to a place prepared by God. There she is
taken care of for 1260 days (12:1-6). A second time
the dragon pursues the woman in her flight to the
wilderness where she is to be nourished for "a time, and
times, and half a time" (12:13,14), a phrase which *The
New English Bible* translates: "for three years and a
half."

Three prominent Old Testament stories figure in the
formation of these scenes. John apparently expects the
viewers of his pictures to be familiar with all three of
them. The first is the story of Moses and the plagues
in Egypt at the time of the Exodus, although no time
limit is specified in connection with this formative
event in the history of Israel.

The second story is that of Elijah and the drought in
Israel at the time of Elijah's encounter with Ahab and
Jezebel. In 1 Kings 17:1 Elijah minces no words in the
presence of king Ahab: "As the Lord the God of Israel
lives, before whom I stand, there shall be neither dew
nor rain these years, except by my word." The drought
is about to be lifted as the word of the Lord comes to
Elijah "in the third year" and says, "Go, show yourself
to Ahab; and I will send rain upon the earth" (1 Kings
18:1). Here the drought appears to have lasted three

necessarily three and one-half years. However,
er tradition the time is given specifically as three
one-half years (Luke 4:25; James 5:17), and John
ites under the influence of this later tradition.

The third story is that of Antiochus Epiphanes in the
Book of Daniel. In Daniel the fourth kingdom, symbolized by a beast too terrible to be described, is ruled
by a king who blasphemes against God, "wears out the
saints of the Most High," and attempts to change the
times and the law (Dan. 7:19–25). These saints fall
into the king's hand "for a time, two times, and half a
time" (7:25). This king is Antiochus Epiphanes, the
notorious persecutor of the Jews in the second century
B.C. At the end of the book Daniel raises the ongoing
question, "How long shall it be till the end of these
wonders?" (12:6). The man clothed in linen swears by
the living God and answers Daniel that it would be
"for a time, two times, and half a time." The end
will be marked by "the shattering of the power of the
holy people" (12:7). Earlier Daniel wrestled with the
question of what the prophet Jeremiah's reference to
the seventy years of captivity really meant (9:1,2). He
receives the word that the seventy years mean seventy
"weeks of years," that is, 490 years. The 490 years are
to be divided into a scheme of seven weeks, sixty-two
weeks, and one week. This last week in the scheme of
seventy weeks, however, is divided into two halves, and
for one-half of that week sacrifice and offering will
cease and the "abomination of desolation" will be set
up by an evil prince (9:24–27). This one-half of the
week-year is three and one-half years, not just any three
and one-half years but specifically those marked by the
persecution of the Jews under Antiochus Epiphanes in
168–165 B.C.

John's references to three and one-half years—either as forty-two months, or as 1260 days, or as a time, and times, and half a time (Rev. 11:2; 11:3; 12:14)—are therefore not so terribly mysterious after all. Under the impact of the Elijah and Daniel stories the three and one-half years become a symbol for the time of special pressure and hardship experienced by God's people. The greater the pressure, the greater the need for endurance, and the Patmos prophet wants his Asian Christians to endure. Let the past of Elijah and Daniel teach the present.

FINALITY

The time has come for the interlude to fade into the final and climactic part of the vision of the trumpets. Announced as something special, the seventh trumpet turns out to be what was anticipated. The trumpet sounds, and what happens is so special that it functions as the heart of the book. The trumpet blows, and the heavens ring with the cry: "The kingdom of the world has become the kingdom of our Lord and of his Christ, and he shall reign for ever and ever" (11:15).

God and his Christ have the last word. This is what apocalyptic is all about, at least as understood by John. This is the message of the book of Revelation. All the rest is the staging and the form of it. No matter what it may look like or feel like when evil holds the throne —in the person of Antiochus or Nero or Domitian (and the procession continues long past John's day and appears destined to continue long past our own day)— through it all the seventh trumpet sounds its word of finality. This is final: God and his Messiah have the last say.

7

BEASTS AND CHURCH

We have stopped briefly at the mountain top. The seventh trumpet has sounded the final victory. What could possibly top this? The tour should end, but John does not think so. He is no more than half through. The progression of calamities has only gone from one-fourth (6:8) to one-third (8:7–12). More directly, a third woe has been announced as coming soon (11:14), and the seventh trumpet could not have been that woe. Finality does not come easily, no matter how much we may wish for it. To confront a compromising patriotism with political realism John presents his paintings in room six. War between dragon and church (chapter 12) merges into war between beasts and church (chapter 13). A reminder of the 144,000 in true worship leads to a dire warning against false worship and a call for endurance (14:1–13). The scene closes with the double harvest (14:14–20).

DRAGON AND CHURCH

A woman clothed with the sun, her feet on the moon and a crown of twelve stars on her head, gives birth to the Messiah. A big red dragon, foiled in his attempt first to devour the child and then to overcome the woman who gave it birth, continues his war on the rest of the woman's children. While the woman's identity as the mother of Jesus seems at first so obvious as to require no discussion, details in the picture such as the flight into the wilderness require a broader interpretation. The woman represents God's people from whom, to whom, and for whom the Messiah has come.

The war on earth between the dragon and the church has been a serious one from the beginning. The dragon, identified in 12:9 as the Devil and Satan, is bent on the destruction of the Messiah at his birth (not so much a reference to Christmas as to Good Friday). The son, however, escapes to God's throne (the resurrection and ascension). The church by virtue of the woman's flight lives as a wilderness people with the dragon continuing his warfare against them.

The dragon and Michael fight their war in heaven. In his only other appearance in the New Testament Michael is the archangel fighting with the devil over the body of Moses (Jude 9). John has given us no more than Michael's name. The war results in the dragon's defeat and expulsion. Thereupon a loud voice in a repeat of the seventh trumpet proclaims finality: "Now the salvation and the power and the kingdom of our God and the authority of his Christ have come" (12:10). That the victory over the dragon does not come easily John clarifies at once: "And they have conquered him by the blood of the Lamb and by the word of their testimony, for they loved not their lives even unto death" (12:11). John never heard of cheap grace.

However much the dragon was forced to give up by his expulsion from heaven, he has not lost his power to fight. It does not prove immediately fruitful to try to fit the various pieces of the picture into a neat pattern of time and space. How does the middle paragraph describing the war in heaven (12:7–12) fit into the first (12:1–6) and third (12:13–17) which present the war on earth? When in time and where in space was the devil expelled? Or when and where will the expulsion yet happen? Apparently the symbol has something else in mind. It describes what happens all the time and everywhere. The dragon has power, but a power which is limited—particularly since his failure against the Messiah.

BEASTS AND CHURCH

The fight with the church continues, but now the dragon is replaced by two beasts (chapter 13). Beast number one is a composite, hardly to be visualized, of the four animals in Daniel 7 symbolizing four kingdoms. John has chosen to present the features of these four animals in reverse order (13:1,2) to form his picture of the Roman empire with its great power to make war on the saints and to conquer them (13:7). Manuscript evidence, however, leaves the original text of 13:7 somewhat uncertain. The power of Rome is great but, like that of the dragon, limited; it lasts for forty-two months (13:5).

Beast number two exercises the authority of beast number one (13:12). He represents religious subservience to the Roman state, a priesthood in the service of emperor worship. The economic oppression (13:17) which accompanies this alliance of political, military, and religious powers appears as up-to-date as the latest "join the party or else!" or as modern as the squeeze put on by multinational corporations.

Survival depends upon being stamped with "the name of the beast and the number of its name." The number is 666 (13:18). Of various possibilities the most likely still is that the number stands most directly for Emperor Nero. By assigning numerical values to letters of the Hebrew alphabet and turning the Greek name Neron Kaisar into Hebrew script we come up with 666. Another manuscript tradition gives the number instead as 616; turning the Latin Nero Caesar into Hebrew we get 616. The immediate reference to Nero, however, need not exhaust the scope of the symbol. Number 666 continues to march through history with a heavy boot. Too close a look could prove embarrassing. At least one writer has confessed his hesitation to explore the matter any further lest the number turn out to be his own name.[13]

The reference to being stamped by the state leads directly into the picture of the 144,000 on Mount Zion who have their own distinguished mark, the name of the Lamb and of God, on their foreheads (14:1–13). The sound of a new song, a liturgy known only to the 144,000, gives way before the loud cry of the angel with an eternal gospel for the earth dwellers. This gospel proclaims judgment, and calls for authentic worship (14:7) over against the idolatrous worship of the beast (14:9). For the first time (with more to follow in chapter 18) we hear about the fall of Babylon the great (14:8).

With the call for the endurance of the saints (14:12) still ringing in our ears we move to the picture of the double harvest. One like a son of man, seated on a white cloud and crowned in gold, swings his sickle and the earth is harvested like a crop of wheat (14:14–16).

Another angel swings a second sickle, and grapes of the earth are gathered for squeezing in "the great wine press of the wrath of God" (14:17–20). The wheat harvest represents the saving of the faithful while the gathering of the grapes symbolizes the judgment of the wicked.

PATRIOTISM

John has painted a scene dominated by the unholy trinity of the dragon (mentioned eleven times in chapters 12 and 13) and the two beasts (mentioned sixteen times in chapter 13). We meet the dragon again as dragon in 16:13 and as both dragon and devil in 20:2. In the New Testament only the Book of Revelation refers to a dragon. The word beast occurs twenty-two more times in Revelation. In 11:17 we saw a beast coming up from the abyss to wage his war against the two witnesses. In chapter 17 we will meet the scarlet beast ridden by a majestic harlot. Very likely these two beasts stand for beast number one of our present picture (13:1–10).

The closing years of the reign of Emperor Domitian (A.D. 81–96) became a time of mounting pressure on the Christians. The emperor dared to order that he be addressed as Dominus et Deus, Lord and God. As one scholar puts it, Domitian became "the first emperor to wage a proper campaign against Christ; and the church answered the attack under the leadership of Christ's last apostle, John of the Apocalypse."[14]

To express the villainy of Domitian John chose the beast Nero of three decades earlier. By selecting the imagery of the dragon and the beasts John shows himself a patriot of a special kind. When the picture of the beast is applied only to the enemy, real or imagined, or deliberately created for one's own political purposes, and is never applied to one's own abuse of power, it turns patriotism into jingoism. Applied to any and all power gone wrong, including one's own, the picture can put patriotism to its severest test. Who then is Lord, Christ or Caesar? Who wields the final sickle, the arm of the state or the arm of God?

8

NEW EXODUS

The sickles have done their work. The crop has been harvested and the grapes gathered. Again it would seem that the time to stop has come, but John opens the door to yet another room and discloses his amazing picture of the seven last plagues (15:1).

We are standing by another Red Sea. The people of another Exodus have crossed safely to the other side and are singing their song of victory over their persecutor the beast. As the picture of answered prayer introduced the seven trumpets (8:2–5) so now the song of Moses and the Lamb introduces the seven plagues (15:2–16:1).

PLAGUES AND WRATH

The first four of these plagues (16:2–9) belong to the world of nature. Paralleling the first four trumpets, the bowls of wrath are emptied on the land, sea, rivers, and sun. They bring plagues of sores, blood, and scorching heat, clear reminders of the plagues of Egypt at the time of Moses and Pharaoh. The next three plagues (16:10–21) belong more to the world of politics. The bowls are poured out on the throne of the beast, on the river Euphrates, and in the air. They bring plagues of darkness and pain, the assembly for the battle of Armageddon, and finally the many-sided affliction of earthquake, hail, and cup of wrath for Babylon the great.

Two themes dominate John's picture: plagues and wrath. Of the twenty-two references to plagues in the New Testament, sixteen are found in the Book of Revelation, six of them in our present scene. Of the eighteen references to wrath in the New Testament, ten occur in Revelation, four of them in the present context. As he paints his picture of the New Exodus, John weaves together these six references to plagues and the four to wrath.

The vision itself is a great and marvelous sign or portent, seven angels with seven last plagues (15:1). They are the last because with them the wrath of God comes to an end (15:1). Victorious Christians (the martyrs) praise the power and justice of God in their song of Moses and the Lamb. When they have finished their singing, the seven angels with the seven plagues come out of the temple (15:6). Thereupon one of the four living creatures hands to the seven angels seven golden bowls filled with the wrath of God (15:7), and the temple is filled with smoke from the glory and power of God barring entrance to it until the seven plagues of the seven angels are over (15:8). Nothing happens until a loud voice from the temple orders the seven angels to empty their seven bowls of the wrath of God on the earth (16:1). In 16:9 God, who has power over the plagues, ends up by being cursed. With the emptying of the seventh bowl God remembers Babylon to make her drink the cup of his wrath (16:19), and people curse God because of the plague of hail (16:21).

Three additional details warrant mention. Though

alluded to a number of times, Moses is mentioned by name in the Book of Revelation only here. The place name Armageddon occurs only here in the entire New Testament (16:16). The political enemies of the gospel assemble for battle at Armageddon (the "hill of Megiddo") on the great day of God.

Noteworthy in this series is the total devastation. We are no longer dealing with the "one-fourth" of the seals and the "one-third" of the trumpets. Now the blood of the sea kills "every" living thing in it (16:3). At the end of the picture "every" island has vanished and "no" mountains can be found anymore (16:20). Does this progression of the bowls over the seals and trumpets mean what it seems to mean, that history moves in different cycles? Or does it mean repetition or recapitulation, that history goes through the same cycles? Probably both are true. The cycles do represent movement but not unique stages. They are successive, but at the same time a returning again to the beginning, a symbol of the ongoing story of apocalypse and cover-up.

The plagues of Egypt and the Exodus from it at the time of Moses marked the end of Pharoah as the persecutor. Now these plagues and a New Exodus mark the end of Babylon (Rome), the current persecutor. Wrath has entered our vocabulary. God is not to be trifled with. Most immediately he exercises his wrath on behalf of the church. The point of this symbol of the bowls is "neither the collapse of the physical universe nor the punishment of individual men for their contribution to the world's iniquity . . . but the ending of persecution through the removal of the persecutor."[15] This does not mean that other persecutors did not arise and will not continue to arise to join the long procession.

THE NUMBER SEVEN

The seven bowls are the last (15:1), but surely not in the sense that with them John has come to the end of his book. They are, however, the last in the four distinct series of seven churches, seals, trumpets, and bowls. Considerably more than half of the New Testament's uses of the number seven occur in its last book. As we prepare to leave room number seven for the remaining two rooms of pictures it is appropriate to pause before the number seven itself as a structural feature of the Book of Revelation.

The arrangement of the material according to seven letters to seven churches, the opening of seven seals, the blowing of seven trumpets, and the emptying of seven bowls of wrath has stood out so clearly that we could not possibly have missed it. In addition we have heard seven thunders following the shout of the mighty angel (10:3). We have seen the seven spirits of God (1:4; 4:5) and the seven horns and seven eyes of the Lamb (5:6), the great red dragon with seven heads and seven crowns (12:3), and the first beast with ten horns but seven heads (13:1). Next we will see the great whore riding on a scarlet beast with seven heads and ten horns (17:3,7). The seven horns stand for seven hills on which the woman sits (17:9), and also seven kings (17:10–11). All in all there are fifty-some sevens in the book.

We can see for ourselves that with all its interest in the number seven the book can also abandon it in freedom. An arrangement according to seven was far from obvious in the five scenes of heavenly worship in chapters 4 and 5. A pattern of seven was not clear in the portrayal of the beasts and the church (12:1–14:20).

Neither will it be obvious in the painting of the fall of
Babylon (17:1–19:10) or in the final picture (19:11–22),
where the number twelve takes over. Actually less than
half of the book forms itself around a skeleton of seven.
The conclusion seems clear: John has a definite interest
in the number seven, but he uses the number as something less than the one unifying factor for the entire
composition.

9

THE GREAT CITY BABYLON

The next room turns out to be a wilderness (17:3). As we approach the door leading into it we hear what we can expect to find in it, namely, "the judgment of the great harlot" (17:1). "Judgment," which here enters our vocabulary for the first time, is mentioned no less than seven times in this single vision.

What has been sketched before is now filled in. We heard of the fall of Babylon the great as early as 14:8. As recently as the close of the last scene (16:19) we saw Babylon draining the cup of God's wrath. Now the description of the harlot includes her identification as "the great city" (17:1–18). Two separate paragraphs describe the fall of this city (18:1–8, 21–24). On earth three groups bemoan the fall of the city (18:9–20), while in heaven the response is "Hallelujah!" (19:1–10).

IN ONE HOUR

We are participating in the judgment of Rome. There can be no mistaking the reference to the "seven hills" in 17:9. The interpretation of the beast in 17:8, 11 is not quite this clear; however, he appears to be Emperor Nero, the tyrant of some years past who is still far from forgotten. The king to come will last "only a little while" (17:10), and ten others receive authority with the beast for "one hour" only (17:12).

"In one hour" judgment has come. This is the refrain of the dirge sung over the fall of Babylon in chapter 18. "Fallen, fallen is Babylon the great!" The moment of truth has arrived. The security the city felt was matched by the speed of its downfall: "in a single day" (18:8). Kings, merchants, and seamen mourn her fall, and they are all struck by how suddenly it has come about. All "in one hour"; that's how it happened (18:10,17,19).

Seen on earth as having been destroyed in one hour, Rome has smoke which ascends to heaven forever (19:3). The heavenly celebration of the city's fall becomes the only occasion for using the word "Hallelujah." Contrary to what one may have come to expect from the way Handel's Hallelujah Chorus has sung its way into our language, the word occurs only in this paragraph in the entire New Testament. The four creatures and twenty-four elders sing it once (19:4), and a great multitude sings it three times (19:1,3,6). This same multitude rejoices in the coming wedding celebration of the Lamb and the Bride (19:7) as an angel extends the invitation to the marriage supper (19:9).

TWO CITIES

The "city" is a prominent enough symbol in the Book of Revelation to claim our attention. The noun occurs twenty-seven times, and twelve cities are either named or alluded to (without necessarily being identified as cities). The twenty-seven occurrences of the noun clearly arrange themselves (with one uncertainty) into two clusters of meaning. There is "the great city" and there is "the holy city," and the two are on a collision course. Seven of the twelve named cities we remember as the locations of the seven churches to whom the book is addressed. The additional five cities serve in the first instance as historical examples, but they and other references as well can also carry a heavy symbolic meaning.

The contrast between the two cities in chapter 11 is sharp. "The holy city" is trampled by the nations (11:2). "The great city" has the street where the corpses of the two witnesses lie unburied (11:8).

Around this latter reference (11:8) there cluster the seven usages in our present picture (chapters 17 and 18) which present the city exclusively as the city of woe, the great Babylon which has fallen. Here belong also the city one-tenth destroyed in an earthquake (11:13), the great city split in three (16:19), and the fallen cities of the nations (16:19).

Around the former reference (11:2) there cluster the thirteen usages in chapters 20–22 presenting the city exclusively as the beloved, new, and holy Jerusalem. Here belongs the promise of the name of God's city to be given to the victors of the church of Philadelphia (3:12).

This twofold grouping leaves only the reference to the city in 14:20 unaccounted for. Does the city "outside" of which the wine press is trodden belong to the one category or the other?

Three of the five cities named or alluded to beyond those receiving letters are together in the first group in 11:8 where "the great city" is further identified as "Sodom and Egypt, where their Lord was crucified." Egypt, while not a city, here serves as a symbol of a city, and Jerusalem is referred to in the crucifixion statement. Babylon, the fourth city, is particularly prominent, mentioned six times and always described as "great" and as being under judgment. The fifth city is Rome, not mentioned by name but intended by the reference to the seven hills (17:9) and by the name Babylon. Four of these five cities (Sodom, Egypt, Babylon, and Rome) serve as types of concentrated wickedness. Jerusalem, however, does double duty, belonging to the great city of unfaithfulness (11:8) on the one hand, and enduring as the city of God (3:12; 21:2,10) on the other.

John thus recognizes but two cities, "the great city" and "the holy city." He would seem to have considerable difficulty with the so-called secular city which was in vogue a few years ago. The secular city was not to be feared but celebrated; it was held to be not a secularism which enslaves us but a secularization which sets us free. For John the great city is old and full of woe. The holy city is new and part of the creation yet to come.

SPIRIT OF PROPHECY

Just at the point of leaving room number eight, we spot a detail which requires a closer look: "For the testimony of Jesus is the spirit of prophecy" (19:10). This expression provides the occasion for us to try to understand the prophetic interpretation of the Book of Revelation. Earlier we interpreted the symbol of the three and one-half years historically. We saw it as speaking to the immediate historical situation of the early church —without thereby concluding, however, that the immediate situation exhausted the meaning of the symbol.

Now what happens when temporal data like these are interpreted prophetically? The data then serve as the basis for seeing predictions fulfilled in ongoing history, especially in our own present and immediate future. Of special concern is the use of John's numbers in recurrent attempts to calculate the end of the world.

What is this spirit of prophecy as seen by those who espouse the prophetic as over against the historical interpretation? We can perhaps shed light on the matter by: (1) listing some texts which provide the rationale for this interpretation, (2) giving the most commonly used numerical data, (3) describing the method of calculation, and (4) citing some specific examples.

For many Christians two statements from Jesus are definitive: "But of that day or that hour no one knows, not even the angels in heaven, nor the Son, but only the Father" (Mark 13:32), and "It is not for you to know times or seasons which the Father has set by his own authority" (Acts 1:7). This ends once-for-all any attempt on our part to figure out the calendar of heaven. For others, however, this simply will not suffice. The angels may not know, even Jesus may not know, but we can know by the spirit of prophecy. Four texts, among others, are cited in support: "Surely the Lord God does nothing, without revealing his secret to his servants the prophets" (Amos 3:7); "Knowledge shall increase" and "those who are wise shall understand" (Dan. 12:4,10); "The mystery of God, as he announced to his servants the prophets, should be fulfilled" (Rev. 10:7); and of course there is our present text dealing with the spirit of prophecy (Rev. 19:10).

Four sets of numbers, among others, provide the data. There is first the number seven, seen in the seven days of creation-week, or the "seven times" of Daniel 4:16, or the "sevenfold" of Leviticus 26:18. Secondly, half of seven is three and one-half, most directly the three and one-half years expressed either as "a time, and times, and half a time" (Rev. 12:14; cf. Dan. 7:25; 12:7) or as forty-two months (Rev. 11:2; 13:5) or as 1260 days (Rev. 11:3; 12:6). Thirdly, seventy years give the length of the Babylonian captivity (Jer. 25:11,12; 29:10). Fourthly, the restoration of the sanctuary will take place after 2300 evenings and mornings (Dan. 8:14).

The method of calculation depends on interpretation. The scriptural number itself remains literal, while the unit of time it expresses can vary to fit the interpretive scheme.

By one combination of texts (Ps. 90:4 and 2 Pet. 3:8) the days of creation cease being days and become instead six periods of history of 1000 years each. If, for example, by the chronology of James Ussher (1581–1656) creation began in 4004 B.C., then there were exactly 4000 years of Old Testament history up to the birth of Jesus and there will be exactly 2000 years of New Testament history, bringing the world to an end in A.D. 1996, a total of 6000 years of world history or 1000 years for each of the six days of creation. Another scheme had creation begin in 4070 B.C. Consequently the end of the world was awaited in A.D. 1930.[16]

By another combination of texts, a day functions neither as a day nor as 1000 years but as one year. This important year-day principle grows out of the references to "a day for each year" in Numbers 14:34 and Ezekiel 4:6 as well as the "sevenfold" of Leviticus 26:18 and the "seven times" of Daniel 4:16. These calculations result in a period of 2520 days (seven years times 360 days) or really 2520 years. Some prophetic interpreters see in Daniel 8:14 with its 2300 evenings and mornings neither 1500 days nor even 2300 days but 2300 years.

As we saw earlier, in the Old Testament itself a year can cease being a year by becoming a week-year. In Daniel 9:2, 24–27 the seventy years of Jeremiah are reinterpreted as seventy week-years, that is, seven times seventy or 490 years.

For William Miller (1782–1849), founder of the American Advent movement more than a century ago,[17] there are essentially three steps in the process. First, the crucifixion of Jesus had to take place at the close of the seventy week-years (490 years) of Daniel 9. Secondly, in the margin of the King James Bible used by Miller the date of the crucifixion was given as A.D. 33. Four hundred and ninety minus thirty-three then takes us back to 457 B.C. Again in the margin of the Bible used by Miller 457 B.C. was given as the date of the seventh year of Artaxerxes (Ezra 7:7), interpreted now as the year of the "going forth" in Daniel 9:25. Thirdly, we pick up Daniel 8:14 with its reference to 2300 evenings and mornings preceding the restoration of the sanctuary. The number 2300 stands for years. Twenty-three hundred minus 457 then brings us up to A.D. 1843. Making the necessary adjustments to the Jewish calendar, Miller hit upon October 22, 1844 as the end of the world. When the expected end did not come and Christ did not return to earth as expected, the prophecy was nevertheless deemed fulfilled—and precisely on that October day as Christ for the first time entered the heavenly sanctuary to restore it according to Daniel 8:14.

In a second more recent example,[18] the seven years

times 360 days become 2520 days, again interpreted as years by the year-day principle. We then look for events which are 2520 years apart to find incredible prophecies fulfilled in our day. If Esarhaddon (2 Kings 19:37) is seen as deporting the exiles in 677 B.C., then 2520 minus 677 brings us to A.D. 1843, which when properly adjusted comes to the same result as that of William Miller. If Nebuchadnezzar is seen as succeeding his father in 602 B.C., thereby inaugurating the gentile domination of Palestine, then 2520 minus 602 equals A.D. 1918, the end of World War I and the beginning of the British protection of Palestine as a more gentle gentile domination than that of the Turks. If 590 B.C. is given as the date for the siege of Jerusalem by Nebuchadnezzar, then 2520 minus 590 equals A.D. 1930, the expected end of gentile domination of Palestine and the return of Christ.

Schemes such as these abound, and even where those who propose them do not intend such a precise calendar notation they nevertheless tend to see prophecy being fulfilled in our day. For example, the ten horns of Daniel and Revelation are sometimes interpreted to mean the ten nations of the European Common Market.[19]

One thing can safely be said. Viewers of apocalyptic pictures do not all see the same thing. Some find in them the great excitement and deep certainty of being able to follow God's own timetable of world history. Others see nothing of the kind; to them the prophetic interpretation as such appears to be misguided as to the very nature of prophecy, and arbitrary in the use of biblical texts.

10

NEW CREATION

"Then I saw heaven opened." These words in Revelation 19:11 identify the final room of John's astounding gallery. Here the pictures are arranged in two sections. When the opposition has been removed (19:11–20:15) the new creation takes center stage (21:1–22:5). In this two-part development we find not only an important symbol in its own right but also the structural feature which brings the book to an artistic close.

PRISONERS OF WAR

The lines of the closing battle are clearly drawn (19:11–21). The commander of the armies of heaven rides a white horse. He has many names, one known only to himself, the others known to all who care to know—Faithful and True, Word of God, King of kings and Lord of lords. His armies of the martyrs all in white also ride white horses. The beast and the kings of the earth command the armies of the opposition. So certain is the outcome that before the battle has even begun the birds receive the invitation to gorge themselves on the corpses of the armies of earth. In one of the boldest images in all of biblical literature this becomes "the great supper of God" (19:17).

The battle has wiped out the persecuting troops (19:21). As prisoners of war the beast and the false prophet (who doubled as beast number two in chapter 13) get their sentence to the lake of fire (19:20). The fate of the dragon remains to be told as part of the next picture of the thousand years.

A THOUSAND YEARS

The symbol of the millennium (20:1–10) has aroused great interest in some circles and been variously interpreted. Some dismiss the picture as meaningless; others spiritualize it to mean the entire period of the Christian church on earth; still others take it quite literally even to the extent of having Christ set up his headquarters for 1000 years in the Empire State Building in New York City.

On the text itself several observations can be made:

1. The expression 1000 years occurs very rarely. In biblical and earliest Christian literature we find it only in Psalm 90:4, quoted in 2 Peter 3:8; in the Epistle of Barnabas 15:4, an early Christian work; and six times in Revelation 20:2–7, once in each of the six verses. The Greek word for 1000 is *chilia,* from which we get our English term "chiliasm." The Latin equivalent *mille* has given us our term "millennium."

2. Three times in Revelation 20 (vss. 2, 4, 6) the words occur in a construction used to express duration or extent. We are dealing with an ordinary expression for the duration of time.

3. Three times (vss. 3, 5, 7) the words function as the subject of the verb "to end." The duration will come to an end.

4. Once (vs. 2) the duration refers to Satan bound. The angel chains him up.

5. Twice (vss. 4, 6) the duration refers to ruling with Christ. The martyrs of the first resurrection have this privilege.

6. Twice (vss. 3, 5) the words are part of an "until" clause, designating that which cannot happen during the 1000 years, that is, "until" they are ended. Satan cannot seduce the nations anymore, and the rest of the dead (other than the martyrs) do not come to life until the period is over.

7. Once (vs. 7) the expression belongs to a "when" clause pointing to the end of the period with something yet to follow. "When" the 1000 years are over Satan is set free to seduce the nations into a final battle. Where the prophet Ezekiel (chapters 38 and 39) had identified the enemy from the north as "Gog of the land of Magog," John refers to the nations at the four corners of the earth as "Gog and Magog." The battle ends with the defeat of Gog and Magog, and Satan's sentence to the lake of fire. There he joins his deputies, the two beasts.

On the meaning of this 1000-year period several conclusions seem valid:

1. The 1000 years are described as a duration of time with a distinguishing quality or content, both negative and positive. The negative is the confinement of Satan; the positive is the rule of the martyrs with Christ. Nothing is said about the place of this rule.

2. The duration is marked by both a beginning and an end, the chaining and the freeing of Satan respectively. What precedes this beginning and follows this end receives far more attention in the Book of Revelation than what lies in between. The "millennium" itself plays an extremely minor role in the book as a whole.

3. From the book's overall emphasis on nearness we gather that John expected the "millennium" to come to pass shortly. To conclude because this did not happen that the 1000 years must therefore mean the entire time of the Christian church on earth wherein the saints reign seems to move far from John's intention.

4. As practically everything else in the Book of Revelation, the 1000 years functions as a symbol. The duration of "1000 years" need not be any more the literal time of the calendar than the fall of Rome "in one hour" is the literal time of the stopwatch. The picture embodies within itself two contrasting views of history, neither of which John can deny. On the one hand John sees too much evidence of God at work in history to permit its reduction to nothingness before the coming of God's ultimate rule. On the other hand John sees too much wrong in history to allow it to fade into a final fulfillment without first going through the rigors of judgment. Through the symbol of the millennium we comprehend the truth of both of these views of history, and the tragic error of either view when it ignores the other. There is a way of getting from the old order to the new creation, but it must be a transitional step and a temporary one. To squeeze out of the symbol of the millennium answers to alien questions of place and time is to violate the integrity of the symbol.

DRAWING TO A CLOSE

The 1000 years have ended. Satan has made his last move and has received his sentence. The dead remain to be judged (20:11–15) before we move on to view the picture of new creation. The dead assemble in front of the great white throne to hear the verdict from the book of life. Not only must Death and Hades relinquish their dead, but they in turn end up in the lake of fire to join the hellish trinity of the dragon and his two beasts previously sent there. With the opposition taken care of, John can move to the end of his scroll in a way he could not at the time of the seventh trumpet or the double harvest.

We pause to review the sequence which provides this satisfying structural close to the book. We have moved through the one-fourth and one-third destruction brought by the seals and the trumpets to the total devastation wrought by the plagues. As early as 11:18 we were led to expect an imminent third woe which never seemed to come. Now we have been through it. In 19:20 the two beasts end up in the lake of fire. In 20:10 their leader the dragon joins them there. In 20:14,15 Death and Hades and those not recorded in the book of life are added. In 21:8 sinners of various kinds share the same fate in a final inventory of the opposing forces. In 21:6 the words "It is done!" announce the new creation. Only when the death-dealing forces of the old order have been accounted for in their entirety can the new creation set forth in its fullness. The exhibition of inspired art can now move to its appropriate end. John has proved his artistry to be of the highest order.

NEW CREATION

"Then I saw a new heaven and a new earth" (21:1). At this point, and most appropriately here at the end, the word *new* moves into its honored place. We have heard the word before in a more muffled tone in the new song of 5:9 and 14:3, but now we hear it in the highest register. For the writer of Revelation there can be nothing more new than this. The final crisis has passed and the first heaven and the first earth and the sea have disappeared. The new heaven and the new earth have replaced them.

The symbol begins with the landscape and moves into smaller and more detailed foreground pictures. John presents first the blessedness of life in "the holy city, new Jerusalem" (21:1–8), and then, accepting the angel's invitation to see the Bride, the wife of the Lamb, he portrays in greater detail "the holy city Jerusalem" (21:9–22:5).

In the general view God himself speaks from his throne: "Behold, I make all things new" (21:5), and again, "It is done!" (21:6). In this newness God dwells with people in an intimacy that means no more tears and no more death and an abundance of the water of life for free. It means also the exclusion of others in the judgment of the second death (21:8).

In the detailed pictures the holy city Jerusalem descends from heaven directly from God and shows a fourfold distinctiveness portrayed by John in as many paragraphs. The city has a radiance like that of the rarest jewel (21:9–14), and it has the dimensions of perfection (21:15–21). The city has a glory attracting the nations to bring their own honor and glory into it through the gates which are never shut (21:22–27). Lastly the city has the abundance of the river and tree of life (22:1–5).

THE NUMBER TWELVE

The dominant symbol to express all this is the number twelve, either the number itself or its multiples 144 and 12,000. The wall of the city has twelve gates; at the gates there are twelve angels, and on the gates the

names of the twelve tribes of the sons of Israel (21:12).
The twelve gates are twelve pearls (21:21). The wall
has twelve foundations, and on them are the names of
the twelve apostles of the Lamb (21:14). These foundations are enumerated from one to twelve, each with
its own jewel (21:19,20).

The city lies "foursquare" but is also a cube with
sides of 12,000 stadia (21:16). In nonsymbolic English
this amounts to about 1500 miles. The wall seen by
itself is "a great high wall" (21:12) measuring 144
cubits (21:17). Again in nonsymbolic English this
amounts to a little more than 200 feet, and when set
against the great height of the city itself (1500 miles) it
amounts to hardly more than a line drawn around the
base of the cube. To the abundance of the city, with
its river of the water of life, the tree of life contributes
its twelve kinds of fruits, one kind per month (22:2).

The man of Patmos has been at the privileged gate.
He has seen the radically new, and as he comes to the
pastoral task of putting it into words he finds that nothing serves quite as well as the number twelve. Through
the number twelve we see the continuity and totality
and perfection among God's redeemed people which
alone can properly be called new.

With this climax of newness John has brought us
back to the earlier climax of finality. The vision of
newness closes with the dwellers in the new heaven and
earth in an attitude of worship. Night has become day.
The light of lamp or sun has become superfluous because "the Lord God will be their light" (22:5). This
is new. The trumpet sounds and the heavens resound:
"The kingdom of the world has become the kingdom of
our Lord and of his Christ, and he shall reign for ever
and ever" (11:15). This is final.

CONCLUSION

No one who tours John's gallery will claim at the end to have understood it all. Nevertheless a number of truths have impressed themselves upon us during our brief tour, and we can sum up the dominant ones. Fuller understanding can come only through return viewings of the pictures themselves.

1. Disclosure has come by means of symbols. From the point of view of the writer of Revelation it becomes an inexcusable disparagement to say of a picture that it is *"only* a symbol." John insists that the matter itself is so deep that "only a *symbol*" could possibly reveal it. Symbols have a logic of their own. They call not for a literal visualizing but for a seeing *through* them to experience their emotional power. That apocalyptic symbols can have power none but the most insensitive will deny.

2. We have been confronted by historical realism. There are catastrophes and rigors of judgment in history, but at times it must have seemed that the writer of Revelation was going overboard in giving them so prominent a place in his book. At any rate, John is not an escapist writer. Violation of God's law has its consequences. An impersonal cause-effect relationship

cannot be the full explanation. Judgment remains a fact because God is God; indeed, for this very reason judgment is inescapable.

3. We have also been confronted by political realism. The "powers that be" may not realize it, but there are limits to political authority. When the established Roman authority came to deserve the name "Babylon" John had to see his patriotism in a new way—in intimate relationship with his worship life. Without using the term itself, John, exercising his own responsible citizenship, spoke relevantly to the issue of political ethics.

4. In addition we have seen impressive pictures of the oneness of the universe. There is one universe, but it is both heaven and earth. The first heaven and the first earth are so interlocked that they must both make way for the new heaven and the new earth. Revelation has told us that the universe as we ordinarily see it is one all right, but only half of one. It has at the same time tried to uncover for us something of the other half, about which we know so little.

5. Revelation has also shown forth the finality of God's rule. The kingdoms of the world come and go, one by one, but an everlasting kingdom remains, the kingdom of God and of his Christ. It is God, not some tyrant of whatever stripe, who has the last word. For John there can be no firmer conviction or greater hope than this. It has not been the purpose of John's pictures to disclose the details of place or time or the manner of the last word. They are best left in the hands of God.

NOTES

1. *Time,* 4 August 1967, p. 12.

2. *Life,* 11 August 1967, p. 60.

3. *Time,* 21 September 1970, p. 20.

4. W. Stanley Mooneyham, *What Do You Say to a Hungry World?* (Waco: Word Books, 1975) , p. 173.

5. Walter L. Owensby, "Multinationals: Impact and Accountability," *Church and Society* 66 (January-February 1976) : 31.

6. G. B. Caird, *A Commentary on the Revelation of St. John the Divine* (New York: Harper & Row Publishers, 1966), p. v.

7. Henry B. Swete, *The Apocalypse of St. John* (Grand Rapids: Eerdmans Publishing Co., 1951), p. ccxvii.

8. W. Peters, *Auslegung der Offenbarung St. Johannis* (Zwickau i. S.: Johannes Herrmann, 1899) , pp. 30–87.

9. *Des Moines Register,* 25 September 1967, p. 11.

10. *Saturday Review,* 29 July 1967, p. 26.

11. Paul S. Minear, *I Saw a New Earth* (Washington: Corpus, 1968) , pp. 74–84.

12. Jean-Louis D'Aragon, "The Apocalypse," in *The Jerome Biblical Commentary,* 2 vols., ed. Raymond E. Brown et al. (Englewood Cliffs, N.J.: Prentice-Hall, 1968) , 2:479.

13. Berengaud, a 9th century Latin commentator. See Swete, *The Apocalypse,* p. ccxii.

14. Ethelbert Stauffer, *Christ and the Caesars* (Philadelphia: Westminster Press, 1955) , p. 150.

15. Caird, *A Commentary on the Revelation,* p. 201.

16. John Quincy Adams, *His Apocalypse* (Dallas: The Prophetical Society of Dallas, 1925).

17. LeRoy Edwin Froom, *The Prophetic Faith of the Fathers* (Washington: Review and Herald, 1954), 4: 455–905.

18. Adams, *His Apocalypse,* pp. 75–76.

19. Hal Lindsey, *The Late Great Planet Earth* (Grand Rapids: Zondervan Publishing House, 1970), pp. 94–97.

SUGGESTIONS FOR
FURTHER READING

Caird, G. B. *A Commentary on the Revelation of St. John the Divine.* New York: Harper & Row, 1966.

A competent and perceptive interpretation, the best we have.

Fiorenza, Elisabeth Schüssler. "The Revelation to John," in Gerhard Krodel, ed., *Hebrews, James, 1 and 2 Peter, Jude, Revelation.* Philadelphia: Fortress Press, 1977, pp. 99–120.

A brief but illuminating contribution to the series *Proclamation Commentaries: The New Testament Witnesses for Preaching*; underscores the artistry of John's composition.

Lilje, Hanns. *The Last Book of the Bible.* Philadelphia: Fortress Press, 1967.

Written by a church leader for whom the Domitian of John's day proved to be the Hitler of his own day.

Niles, D. T. *As Seeing the Invisible.* New York: Harper & Brothers, 1961.

Analysis and meditation written as a first guide for those who visit the "wonderful country" of the Book of Revelation.

Stauffer, Ethelbert. *Christ and the Caesars.* Philadelphia: Westminster Press, 1955.

Especially the chapter on Domitian and John sharpens the question of who is Lord for the reader of Revelation.

Stringfellow, William. *An Ethic for Christians and Other Aliens in a Strange Land.* Waco: Word Books, 1973.

Writes with the conviction that contemporary America has much to learn from the Book of Revelation.

94-8-178A NC